Lettuce Turnip the Beet!

Colors, Counting and Corny Jokes from the Farm Market

Compiled and illustrated by Kelly Nogoski

First published by Experience Early Learning Company
7243 Scotchwood Lane, Grawn, Michigan 49637 USA

Text Copyright ©2015 by Experience Early Learning Co.
Printed and Bound in the USA

ISBN 978-1-937954-22-2
visit us at www.ExperienceEarlyLearning.com

At the farm market, there's a lot to see. Count and joke along with me!

1
red apple

When is an apple a grouch?
When it's a crab apple!

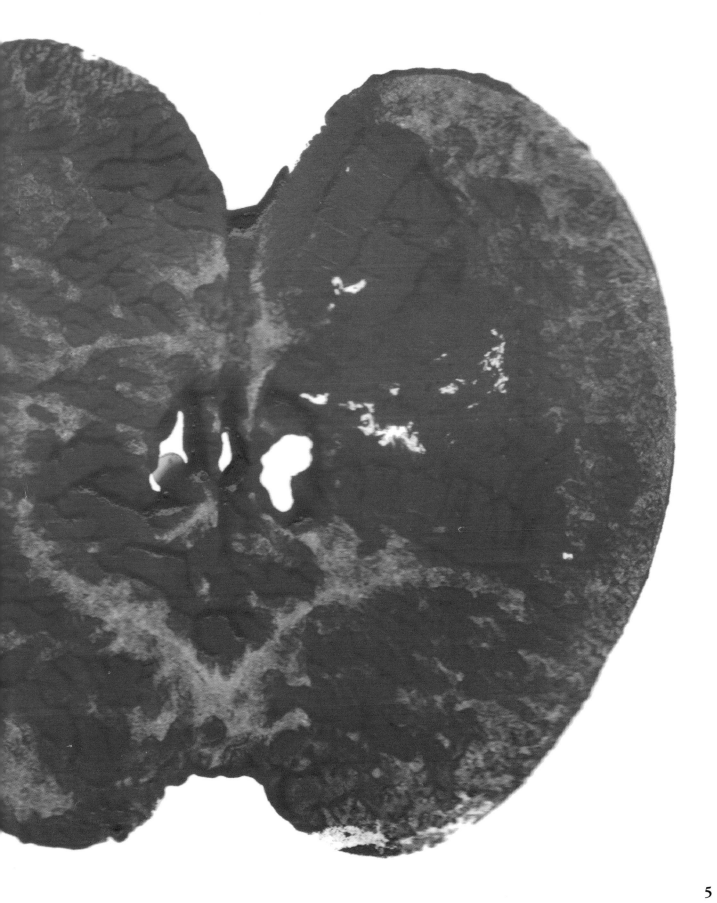

5

2 purple eggplants

Where do eggs grow?

On an eggplant!

3 green heads of lettuce

Knock knock.

Who's there?

Lettuce.

Lettuce who?

Lettuce in. It's cold out here!

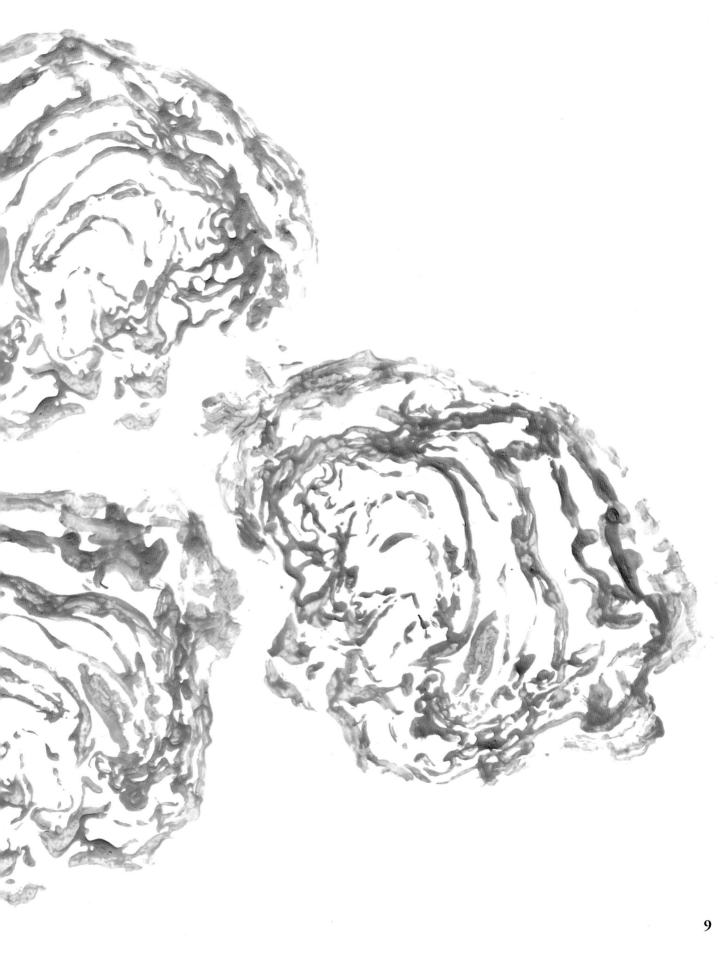

4 yellow bananas

Why did the banana go to the doctor?

Because it wasn't peeling well!

5

green and white leeks

What's the worst vegetable
to serve on a boat?

Leeks!

6
yellow ears
of corn

Why shouldn't you tell secrets
in a cornfield?

There are too many ears!

7 purple beets

Why do people dance to the vegetable band's music?

It has a good beet!

8 red tomatoes

What did the fast tomato say to the slow tomato?

Ketchup!

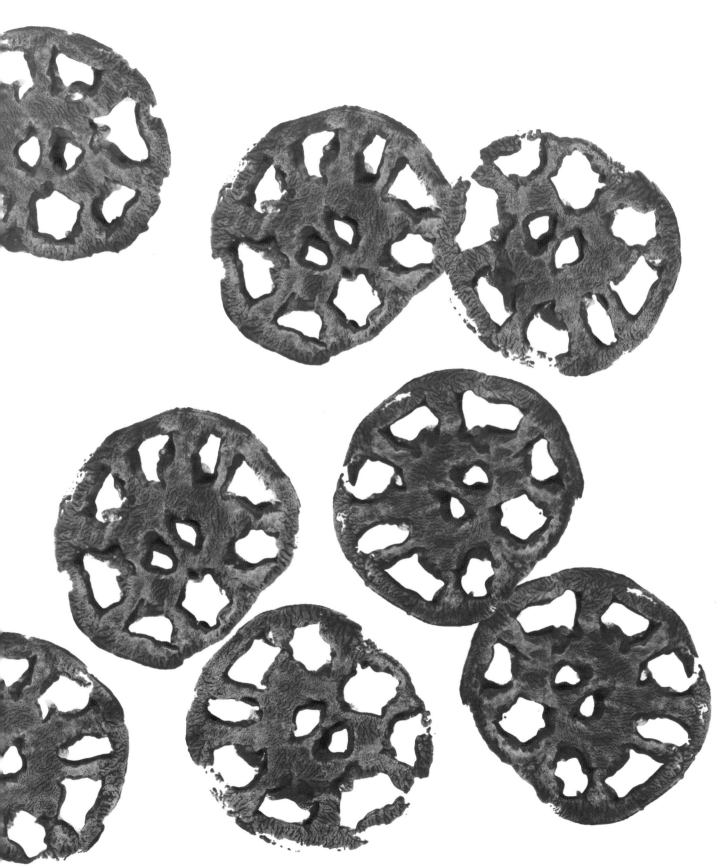

9 green zucchini

What kind of vegetable likes to look at animals?

Zoo-chini!

10
white and purple turnips

Knock knock.

Who's there?

Turnip.

Turnip who?

Turnip the music. I love this song!

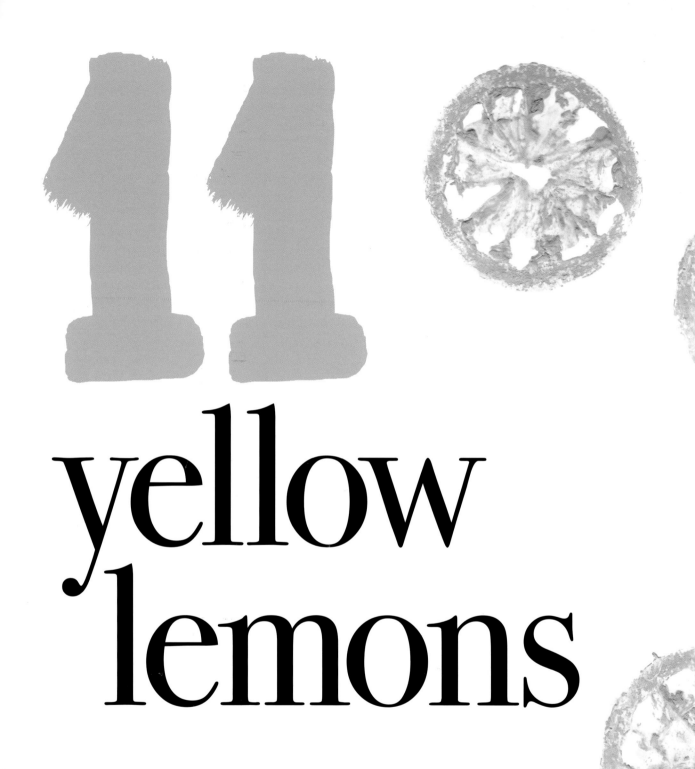

11 yellow lemons

What do you give a sick lemon?

Lemon aid!

12
orange carrots

How do you find a lost rabbit?

Make a noise like a carrot!

13

green kiwi

What's green and goes down
a mountain?

A skiwi!

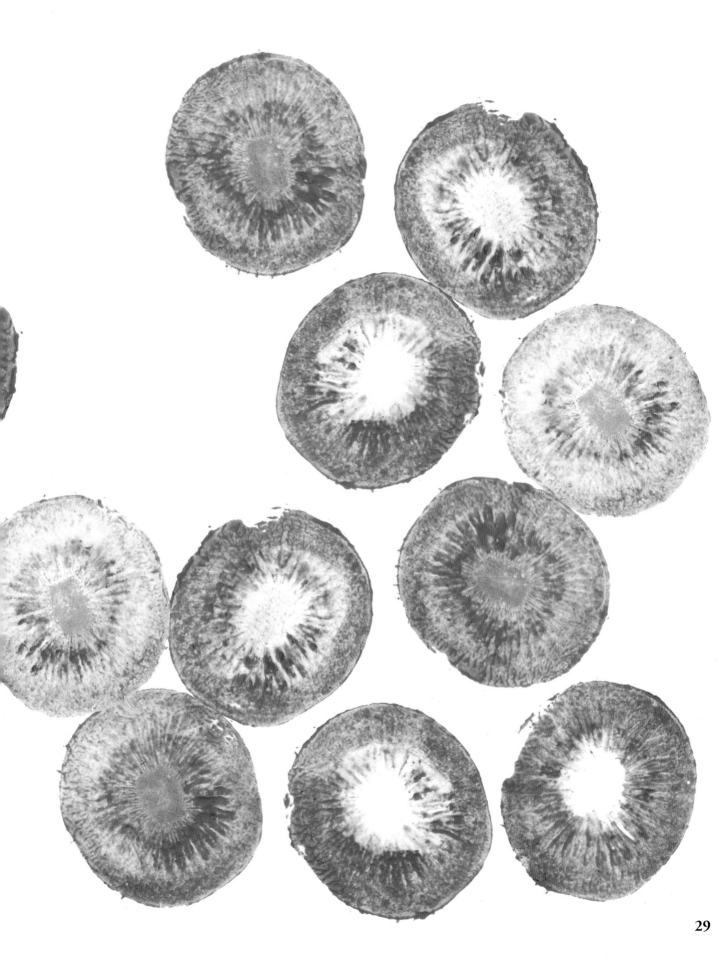

14
yellow starfruit

What fruit comes out at night?

Starfruit!

15
green leaves of spinach

What's a dancer's favorite vegetable?
Spin-ach!

33

16
white mushrooms

What room can be eaten?

A mushroom!

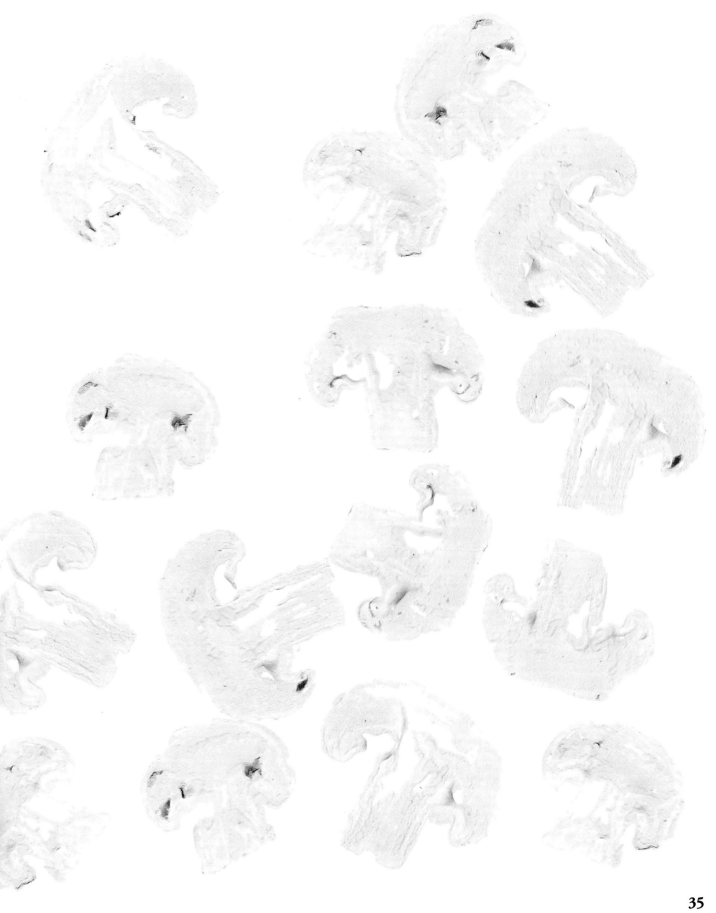

17
green grapes

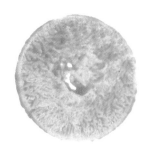

Why aren't grapes ever lonely?

Because they come in a bunch!

18
red strawberries

Why were the strawberries upset?

Because they were in a jam!

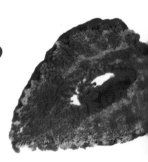

19
green pieces of celery

What does celery wear to stay warm?

Stalkings!

20
blue blueberries

What's the scariest fruit?
Boo-berries!

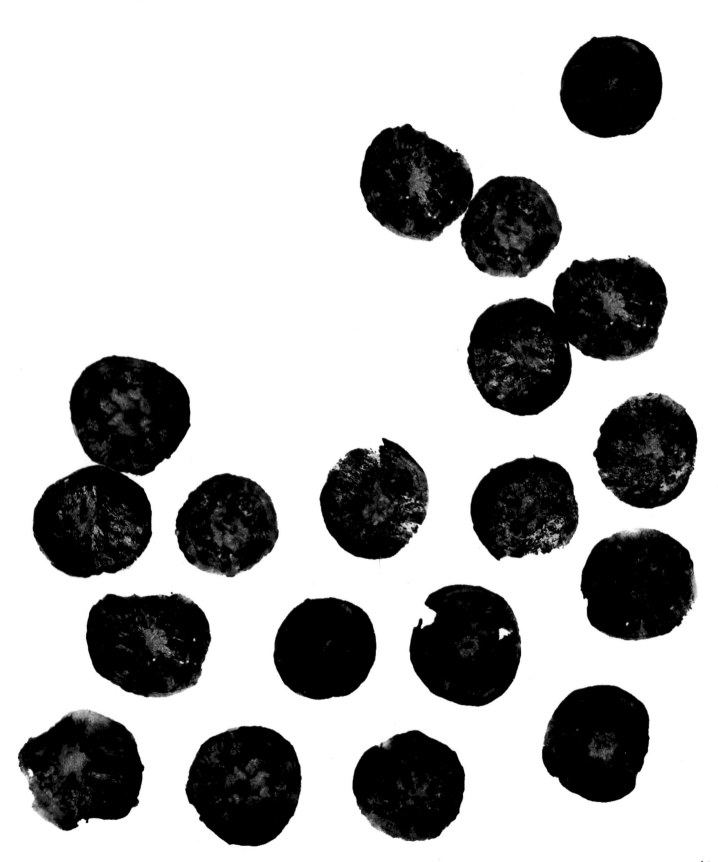

What fun,
all this produce,
a fresh, tasty treat!
What would be
the first you'd eat?